Copyright © 2024 by Andrea Marie Wady and AERDNA EIRAM
A division of Redefine Injection Concierges Inc.

All rights reserved. No part of this publication may be reproduced, distributed, or transmitted in any form or by any means, including photocopying, recording, or other electronic or mechanical methods, without the prior written permission of the author, except in the case of brief quotations embodied in critical reviews and certain other noncommercial uses permitted by copyright laws.

Printed in the United States of America

For inquiries regarding the use of this article, booking the author for speaking engagements, and private-label skincare brand consulting services, please contact the author directly.

Email: Inquiry@aerdnaeiram.com
Website: https://www.aerdnaeiram.com

Table of Contents

Introduction: Welcome to Your Brand-Building Journey	9
Chapter 1: Discovering Your Unique Brand Idea	15
Chapter 2: Developing Your Brand Identity	22
Chapter 3: Designing Your Product or Service	30
Chapter 4: Building a Brand Development Plan	38
Chapter 5: Developing a Cohesive Brand Aesthetic	48
Chapter 6: Preparing for Production	56
Chapter 7: Building Your Digital Presence	65
Chapter 8: Launching Your Brand	73
Chapter 9: Scaling and Growing Your Business	80
Chapter 10: Navigating Regulatory Compliance and Certification for Custom Formulation and Private Label Products	88
Chapter 11: Staying True to Your Brand	96
Chapter 12: Conclusion - The Ongoing Journey of Entrepreneurship	102

Dedication

To every visionary who dares to dream and believes in the power of turning an idea into something meaningful—this book is for you.

To the aspiring entrepreneurs ready to take that first bold step, and to the seasoned professionals looking to reinvent and elevate their brands, may you find in these pages the inspiration, guidance, and tools to build something extraordinary that truly reflects your unique passion and purpose.

To my Texas roots—from the small-town grit of Longview to the big-city determination of Houston and now Dallas, Texas—you have shaped who I am, instilling in me the courage, resilience, and unwavering belief that hard work and heart can transform any vision into reality.

To the creators, beauty industry innovators, wellness advocates, and product developers who pour their soul into what they do, may you always remember that your mark matters. This journey, with all its challenges and triumphs, is yours to own.

And finally, to my clients, colleagues, and every entrepreneur who has trusted me to help shape their dreams, each of you continues to inspire me every day. Together, we're building more than brands. We're creating legacies.

With Respect and Admiration,

Love Always,

Andi "Andrea Marie Wady — Bachelor of Science in Healthcare Administration, Life Coach, Licensed Esthetician, Cosmetic Injector, Micropigmentation Practitioner, Custom Formulation and Private Label Brand Consultant, Cosmeceutical Formulator, Educator, Author, Speaker, and Founder of AERDNA EIRAM a division of Redefine Injection Concierges Inc.

From Idea 2 Inventory

DESIGN, DEVELOP, AND LAUNCH YOUR BRAND, YOUR WAY

"ANDI" ANDREA MARIE WADY
BSHA, LE, LC, CI, MPS
CUSTOM FORMULATION &
PRIVATE LABEL BRAND CONSULTANT

About the Author

I'm "Andi" Andrea Marie Wady, author, entrepreneur, business and brand consultant, and founder of AERDNA EIRAM, based in Dallas, Texas. My diverse background, which spans writing, real estate, collegiate education, healthcare, beauty, wellness, and hospitality, provides a unique perspective and fuels my mission to support entrepreneurs in turning their visions into reality.

As the founder of AERDNA EIRAM, I've paved a pathway that offers a wide range of specific business services that position our clients to break into their chosen industry strong and equip to soar in the most competitive market spaces.

Through every step of their start-up business development, product creation, and brand building journey, AERDNA EIRAM helps lay the foundation for their business and products debut.

My passion for beauty, wellness, hospitality, and self-expression led me to specialize in developing start-up businesses for entrepreneurs that aim to strengthen their business model by offering products that rival household name brands we've grown to crave.

Whether developing a wellness supplement line, an organic skincare brand, or a cosmetics line, I understand the intricate regulatory environments and technicalities involved, especially when ensuring products meet FDA, USDA, and all other industry standards.

With this book, I hope to inspire fellow entrepreneurs to embrace their vision, trust the process, and confidently build their businesses and brands—knowing that anything is possible with dedication and the right guidance.

Preface

In today's fast-paced and ever-evolving marketplace, the journey from idea to a successful brand is both an exciting and challenging endeavor. As someone who has navigated this intricate path, I understand the complexities that come with transforming a vision into a tangible product. *From Idea 2 Inventory: Design, Develop, and Launch Your Brand, Your Way* is born from my passion for empowering aspiring entrepreneurs and established professionals to embrace their creativity and realize their dreams.

Throughout my career, I have had the privilege of working with a diverse array of clients in the beauty, wellness, and hospitality industries. These experiences have taught me that building a brand is a deeply personal journey. It requires not only a clear vision and unwavering determination, but also a solid foundation of knowledge and practical strategies. This book is designed to be your branding companion and to simplify executing the complex process of the brand-building process, from the initial spark of inspiration to the successful launch of your product.

In the pages that follow, you will find valuable insights on discovering your unique brand idea, developing a cohesive brand identity, and designing products that resonate with your target audience. Each chapter is structured to provide practical guidance, ensuring that you not only understand the theoretical aspects of branding but also gain actionable steps to implement in your own journey.

The journey of entrepreneurship is not without its challenges. However, with perseverance and the right guidance, you can overcome obstacles and embrace the fulfillment that comes with creating a brand that is uniquely yours. As you embark on this journey, I encourage you to reflect on your aspirations and trust in your ability to turn them into reality.

I hope that *From Idea 2 Inventory* inspires you to take that first step, to explore the depths of your creativity, and to launch your brand with confidence. Your vision matters, and the world is waiting to see what you can create.

Here's to your journey—may it be filled with discovery, growth, and success.

Introduction: Welcome to Your Brand-Building Journey

Starting your own brand is one of the most exciting and rewarding challenges you can undertake. Whether you're an aspiring entrepreneur with a passion project, or a seasoned professional looking to take control of your own destiny, this journey is filled with endless possibilities. But like any adventure, it can be daunting. There will be obstacles to overcome, lessons to learn, and decisions to make that will shape the future of your brand. The purpose of this book is to guide you through each step of this process from your initial idea to launching a fully developed product or service into the world.

This chapter sets the stage for your brand-building journey by laying out the framework for what's to come. It will prepare you to think like an entrepreneur and understand the mindset you'll need to build a successful, sustainable brand that aligns with your vision and values.

What is Brand Development?

Brand development is more than just creating a product or service—it's about shaping an experience, a reputation, and a story that resonates with your audience. Your brand represents how individuals perceive both you and your business, serving as the bridge that connects you to your customers. This is what renders you unforgettable.

At the heart of effective brand development lies the capacity to articulate your purpose, pinpoint your audience, and craft a concise message that clearly communicates who you are and what values you uphold. This process requires a blend of creativity, strategic thinking, and implementation. Although each brand possesses its distinct identity, the fundamental elements remain constant: authenticity, consistency, and meaningful connection.

Why Entrepreneurship is Empowering

Embracing entrepreneurship signifies taking charge of your own destiny. It involves actualizing your aspirations, seizing control over your future, and recognizing the worth you contribute to society. The directives or visions of others no longer bind you; instead, you become the architect of your own path, making pivotal decisions, establishing your course, and setting the rhythm for your journey.

For many individuals, the motivation to launch a brand arises from a profound personal aspiration to create something impactful, to escape the limitations of conventional employment, or to harness their skills and passions in a manner that fosters both freedom and satisfaction. Entrepreneurship goes beyond mere financial gain; it is fundamentally about having a purpose. By developing your brand, you are crafting an entity that embodies your core values, interests, and aspirations for what lies ahead in the future.

While this journey can be fraught with obstacles, challenges will inevitably arise—the benefits significantly outweigh these trials. As you progress through this book, you will discover that armed with the appropriate mindset and resources, you can confront each challenge with assurance and tenacity.

What You Will Learn in This Book

This book is designed to walk you through the entire brand creation process, from ideation to inventory. Each chapter will provide actionable insights, practical advice, and tools to help you take your brand from a mere concept to a fully realized product or service ready for market.

Here's an overview of what you can anticipate:

1. **Identifying and Developing Your Brand Idea**
This initial phase focuses on uncovering your distinct brand identity. We will assist you in recognizing your passions, defining your target audience, and strategically positioning your brand to differentiate it from competitors. Additionally, we will delve into market research techniques and the creation of a compelling brand narrative that resonates with your intended audience.

2. **Designing Your Brand and Product**
After solidifying your concept, the next step is to develop your product or service. You will gain insights into creating offerings that align with your brand identity, sourcing high-quality materials, and conducting thorough testing prior to market introduction. Furthermore, we will discuss packaging design and establishing a visual identity that reflects your brand's core values.

3. Developing a Cohesive Brand Strategy

Establishing a brand goes beyond mere product creation; it encompasses the overall experience. You will learn how to formulate a robust brand strategy that includes devising pricing models and crafting marketing plans aimed at fostering customer connections. We'll emphasize the significance of maintaining brand consistency across all interactions.

4. Launching Your Brand

As you prepare to introduce your brand to consumers, having a well-structured launch plan is critical. This section of the book guides you in developing an effective launch strategy—covering tactics for generating excitement, engaging with audiences, and maximizing visibility on launch day. We'll explore partnership opportunities, social media utilization, and public relations strategies to promote your new venture.

5. Building for Longevity and Growth

The introduction of your brand marks just the beginning of its journey. We will examine ways to establish a sustainable business model while analyzing customer feedback and facilitating growth over time. You'll discover how to remain faithful to your brand values while adapting to market shifts and expanding your range of offerings.

The Mindset for Success

One of the critical elements in successfully establishing a brand is the mindset. This book serves not merely as a practical resource but also as a manual for cultivating the right mental approach. Your psychological perspective is equally important as the actions you undertake throughout your journey. Here are several essential principles to consider:

- **Resilience**
Entrepreneurship inherently involves navigating numerous highs and lows. Embracing challenges and setbacks as integral components of your journey will propel you forward. Each obstacle presents an opportunity to learn, grow, and enhance your brand.

- **Flexibility**
While it is vital to have a definitive vision, adaptability is equally crucial. The business environment is perpetually evolving, and your capacity to pivot and innovate will serve as a significant advantage. Occasionally, what you initially set out to accomplish may transform into something more profound than you initially envisioned.

- **Passion and Purpose**
Your enthusiasm acts as the driving force behind your brand's achievements. Maintaining a connection to your underlying

motivations will sustain your momentum during difficult periods. Ultimately, creating a brand that embodies your values and imparts meaning to your life represents the highest reward.

What Success Looks Like

Success in brand development can manifest in various ways. For some individuals, it may signify achieving a particular financial target, while for others, it represents the fulfillment derived from establishing a brand that positively influences society. Regardless of how you define success, this book is designed to guide you on your journey toward realizing your aspirations.

At its core, this endeavor revolves around creating something significant. It involves channeling your creativity, cultivating a legacy, and actualizing your vision. Whether your brand evolves into a widely recognized name or remains an enterprise fueled by passion serving a dedicated clientele, your success will be evaluated based on how effectively your brand embodies your identity and your contributions to your community.

Your Next Step

Now that you have a better understanding of what this journey entails, it is time to immerse yourself in the process. In the following chapters, you'll find detailed guidance, real-world examples, and the tools you need to take the next step toward creating your own brand. Each chapter is structured to provide inspiration and practical advice so that by the end of this book, you'll have everything you need to go from idea to inventory, your way.

Are you ready to start building your brand? Let's begin!

Chapter 1: Discovering Your Unique Brand Idea

Every successful brand starts with a great idea, but a great idea alone isn't enough. You need to dig deeper to create a brand that stands out in the marketplace. This process starts with identifying your passion and purpose, gaining insight into the market environment you are entering, and narrowing down the audience you want to serve. These essential components will guide your business's trajectory and transform your brand into more than just a product— it will become an experience that resonates deeply with your target demographic.

In this chapter, we will explore the steps to help you define a clear, purposeful brand idea aligned with your passion, informed by the market, and tailored to your ideal audience.

Identifying Your Passion and Purpose

Before diving into the practical aspects of brand building, starting with the "why" behind your idea is essential. Why are you starting this brand? What drives you? What problem are you passionate about solving? Your passion is the energy that fuels your business, while your purpose is the underlying reason your brand exists.

Questions to Ask Yourself

Start by asking yourself a few key questions to get clarity on your passion and purpose:

- **What are my personal interests and values?**
Your brand should reflect what excites and inspires you. Whether it's fashion, beauty, wellness, or technology, identifying your personal interests can help point you in the direction of a brand idea that feels authentic and sustainable.

- **What problems am I solving?**
Great brands often solve specific problems or address unmet needs in the market. What challenges or frustrations do you see in your industry? How can your brand offer a solution that hasn't been fully explored?

- **What legacy do I want to create?**
Think about the long-term impact of your brand. Do you want to empower others, make a positive social or environmental difference, or simply create something that reflects your creativity? Understanding the larger vision for your brand helps shape its values and mission.

Example:

- If you're passionate about clean beauty and sustainability, your brand's purpose might be to offer eco-friendly, cruelty-free cosmetics that don't compromise performance. This clearly defined purpose can help guide every decision, from the types of ingredients you use to the way you package and market your products.

Researching the Market and Competition

Once you've identified your passion and purpose, it's time to conduct thorough research into your chosen industry. Understanding market trends, customer needs, and your competition will help you position your brand in a relevant and unique way.

Step 1: Understanding Industry Trends

Start by looking at broader industry trends. What's happening in your sector, and how are consumer preferences shifting? Keeping a pulse on the trends helps ensure your brand stays ahead of the curve.

Key areas to monitor include:

- **Current and Emerging Trends:** Identify what is gaining popularity within your industry. For instance, the wellness sector is increasingly embracing concepts such as mindfulness, mental health awareness, and holistic self-care practices.

- **Customer Expectations:** Assess what consumers currently desire. Are they emphasizing sustainability, convenience, luxury, or cost-effectiveness?

- **Innovative Technologies:** Explore new technologies transforming product or service delivery methods. An example of this can be seen in the fashion industry, where AI-driven personalization is on the rise.

Step 2: Analyzing the Competition

Conducting a competitive analysis allows you to see what's already being offered and identify gaps in the market that your brand can fill. Look at both direct and indirect competitors to get a comprehensive understanding.

Key areas to explore when analyzing your competition:

- **Brand Positioning**: How are your competitors positioning themselves? Are they focused on luxury, affordability, innovation, or customer service?

- **Product Offerings**: What types of products or services are they providing? How can yours stand out?

- **Brand Messaging and Story**: What narratives are they telling, and how are they connecting with their audience? Are they highlighting sustainability, quality, or something else?

- **Strengths and Weaknesses**: Identify your competitors' strengths and weaknesses. What do they do well, and where do they fall short?

This insight can help you carve out a unique space in the market.

Example:

If you're looking to launch a new line of fitness apparel, you might find that the market is saturated with big brands that focus on style and performance. However, by researching consumer preferences, you could identify a growing demand for inclusive sizing or eco-friendly materials, providing an opportunity to differentiate your brand meaningfully.

Defining Your Target Audience

With a clear understanding of your passion, purpose, and the market, the next crucial step is defining your target audience. Knowing exactly who you're creating your brand for allows you to tailor your product offerings, messaging, and marketing strategies to meet their specific needs.

Step 1: Narrowing Down Your Audience

Your target audience isn't "everyone." The more specific you are, the better you can connect with the people most likely to resonate with your brand. Begin by identifying key demographic and psychographic characteristics.

- **Demographics**: These are the statistical traits of your audience, such as age, gender, location, education level, income, and occupation. For example, if your brand creates premium skincare products, you might target women aged 30-75 with a higher income who may be more interested in self-care and anti-aging products.

- **Psychographics**: This focuses on your audience's attitudes, values, and lifestyle choices. What are their interests, hobbies, values, and buying behaviors? Understanding this aspect of your audience will help you connect with them on a deeper emotional level.

Step 2: Identifying Pain Points and Desires

Now that you have a general idea of your target audience, it's important to delve into their pain points and desires. What are they struggling with, and what do they want to achieve? Knowing this will help you position your brand as the solution to their problems or the answer to their needs.

To identify pain points and desires, ask yourself:

- **What problem does my product or service solve?**
For example, if you're launching a sustainable clothing line, your audience might be people who want stylish, eco-friendly options without sacrificing quality.

- **What are my audience's goals?**
Your audience's desires might be to live a healthier, more balanced life or to find products that align with their ethical values.

Understanding these desires will help you create messaging that speaks directly to them.

Step 3: Creating Customer Personas

One of the most effective ways to define your target audience is to create detailed customer personas. These personas represent your ideal customers and serve as a guide for all of your brand decisions. A well-developed persona includes demographic information, behavioral traits, motivations, and challenges.

Example Customer Persona:

- **Name**: Lena
- **Age**: 38
- **Location**: Portland, Oregon
- **Occupation**: Marketing professional working remotely
- **Lifestyle**: Enjoys outdoor activities, yoga, and is conscious of her environmental footprint
- **Pain Points**: Struggles to find high-quality, eco-friendly skincare products that suit her sensitive skin
- **Goals**: Wants to maintain a clean beauty routine that aligns with her values and makes her feel good about her choices.

By understanding Sarah's specific needs and values, you can craft a brand experience that speaks directly to her, ensuring your messaging, product development, and marketing efforts are highly targeted.

Bringing It All Together

Once you've identified your passion, researched the market and competition, and defined your target audience, you're ready to start developing your brand idea in earnest. These foundational steps will be the bedrock for everything you do moving forward. They'll guide your product decisions, branding, marketing strategies, and, most importantly, your ability to connect with your customers in an authentic and impactful way.

Remember, this stage is all about discovery. Take the time to explore different ideas, conduct thorough research, and fine-tune your understanding of who your brand is for and what problem it solves. By doing this upfront work, you'll create a solid foundation that will carry your brand through the next stages of development.

Chapter 2: Developing Your Brand Identity

Your brand identity serves as the public persona of your business. It's how your audience perceives and interacts with you, and it should communicate your brand's values, personality, and purpose in a way that resonates with your target audience. In this chapter, we will delve into the essential components of creating an impactful brand identity. You'll learn how to develop a powerful brand story, define your brand's personality and core values, and make crucial design decisions, like choosing a brand name and logo to differentiate your brand in the marketplace.

Building Your Brand Story

At the heart of every strong brand is a compelling story. A brand story isn't just a biography of your business—it's a narrative that expresses why your brand exists, what it stands for, and how it can positively impact the lives of your customers. When done well, a brand story forms an emotional connection with your audience, drawing them in and making them feel like a part of your journey.

Why a Brand Story Matters

Your brand story serves several important functions:

- **It Humanizes Your Brand**: People don't just buy products; they buy into the story behind them. A great brand story makes your business feel more personal, relatable, and trustworthy.

- **It Creates Emotional Connections**: A well-told story can evoke emotions, which is key to building customer loyalty. When people connect emotionally to your brand, they're more likely to become long-term customers and advocates.

- **It Differentiates You from Competitors**: In a crowded marketplace, a compelling story can set your brand apart. It explains why your brand is unique and why customers should choose you over the competition.

Crafting Your Brand Story

To craft a powerful brand story, start by asking yourself a few key questions:

- **Why did you start your brand?**
The reason behind your brand's creation is often the most compelling part of your story. Was there a problem you wanted to solve, a passion you wanted to pursue, or a gap in the market you identified?

- **What challenges did you face, and how did you overcome them?**
Every entrepreneur's journey comes with challenges. Sharing your struggles and how you overcame them can make your story more relatable and inspiring.

- **How does your brand make a difference in your customers' lives?**
Focus on how your brand adds value. Whether you're offering a solution to a problem, enhancing someone's lifestyle, or promoting a cause, explain how your brand helps your customers in a meaningful way.

Example of a Brand Story

Imagine you're starting a sustainable skincare brand. Here's a sample story:

"I started my skincare journey after struggling for years with sensitive skin and finding that most products were

filled with harsh chemicals. I wanted something natural, effective, and safe for the environment, but the options were limited. So, I set out to create a skincare line made from ethically sourced, all-natural ingredients that people could trust. Today, our products not only soothe sensitive skin but also promote sustainability by using eco-friendly packaging and supporting environmental causes."

This story connects with customers by sharing a personal struggle, offering a solution, and showing how the brand aligns with a larger purpose.

Creating Your Brand Personality and Values

Once you've created your brand story, the next step is to define your brand's personality and values. Your brand personality should encompass humanlike characteristics relatable to your demographic, while your values are the guiding principles that inform how you operate as a business. Collectively, these components influence public perception of your brand and dictate how you engage with your audience.

Developing Your Brand Personality

Think of your brand as a person. How would you describe their personality? Are they playful, fun, professional, authoritative, or bold and rebellious? Your brand's personality will dictate the tone and voice you use in your messaging and marketing.

Steps to Define Your Brand Personality

1. **Consider Your Audience**: What personality type would resonate most with your target customers? For example, if you're targeting young, fashion-forward consumers, a playful and trendy brand personality may be more appealing than a formal one.

2. **Look at Your Brand's Purpose**: Your brand's mission and purpose should align with its personality. You might opt for a sophisticated and elegant personality if your brand focuses on luxury. If it's about eco-friendliness, a caring and conscious personality might be more appropriate.

3. **Choose 3-5 Key Traits**: Narrow your brand's personality down to a few core traits. For example, a fitness brand might choose traits like "motivating," "energetic," and "empowering." These traits should be reflected consistently across all touchpoints, from social media posts to customer service interactions.

Defining Your Brand Values

Your brand values are the core beliefs that guide your business. They shape your decision-making, influence your culture, and provide a moral compass for how you interact with customers and partners.

To define your brand values:

- **Identify What Matters Most to You**: What principles are non-negotiable in your business? Do you prioritize sustainability, integrity, innovation, or community?

- **Think About Your Customers' Values**: Your values should align with what matters most to your target audience. If you're targeting eco-conscious consumers, sustainability should be at the forefront of your brand values.

- **Be Authentic**: Your brand values should be genuine, not just trendy buzzwords. If you claim to value transparency, for example, make sure you live up to that by being open about your business practices and sourcing.

Example of Brand Personality and Values

Imagine a wellness brand with the following personality and values:

- **Personality**: Calm, nurturing, trustworthy, and empowering

- **Values**: Sustainability, ethical sourcing, self-care, and inclusivity

This brand would use soothing language in its marketing, focus on sustainable practices, and empower its customers to take control of their wellness.

Choosing a Name and Logo Design

With your brand story, personality, and values defined, it's time to make some of the most visible decisions for your brand: choosing a name and designing a logo. These elements are the first things your audience will see, so they need to be memorable, representative, and aligned with your overall brand identity.

Choosing the Perfect Brand Name

Your brand name is a critical part of your identity. It should be easy to remember, reflective of your brand's values, and legally available for use. Here are some practical tips for choosing the right name:

1. **Make It Meaningful**: Choose a name that reflects your brand's mission, values, or what you offer. If your brand focuses on organic products, your name could reference nature or purity.

2. **Keep It Simple**: Avoid overly complicated or hard-to-pronounce names. A simple, catchy name is easier for customers to remember and share.

3. **Check Availability**: Make sure the name you choose is available as a domain name for your website and doesn't conflict with any existing trademarks. You can search trademark databases and domain name registries to check.

4. **Think Long-Term**: Consider whether your brand name will still be relevant as your business grows and evolves. Avoid names that are too narrow or specific if you plan to expand your offerings later.

Designing an Impactful Logo

Your logo is the visual symbol of your brand. It must be versatile, recognizable, and reflect your brand's personality. When designing a logo, keep these tips in mind:

1. **Simplicity is Key**: A simple logo is often the most effective because it's easy to recognize and works across different mediums (e.g., websites, packaging, social media). Avoid cluttered designs with too many details.

2. **Choose the Right Colors**: Colors evoke emotions and associations, so select colors that align with your brand's personality. For example, green is often associated with nature and health, while black conveys luxury and sophistication.

3. **Make It Versatile**: Your logo will be used in a variety of contexts, so it needs to look good in different sizes, from small social media icons to large signs. Ensure it's scalable and works in both color and black and white.

4. **Use Symbolism**: If possible, incorporate a symbol that represents your brand's values or

mission. For example, if you're an eco-friendly brand, a leaf or tree could be a meaningful symbol.

Example of Name and Logo

Let's say you're launching an organic skincare brand. You might choose the name **"Pure Earth Skincare Organics"** to reflect the simplicity and purity of your ingredients. Your logo could feature a minimalist design with the silhouette of a woman's face with hair reminiscent of luscious tree leaves and a calming font to communicate your brand's natural, peaceful essence.

Bringing It All Together

Developing your brand identity is about more than aesthetics; it's about creating a cohesive and compelling experience that resonates with your audience on an emotional level. Your brand story sets the tone, your personality and values define how you communicate, and your name and logo give your brand a memorable visual presence.

By dedicating time to strategically developing these components, you establish the groundwork for a robust and long-lasting brand that customers will recognize and connect with.

Chapter 3: Designing Your Product or Service

The heart of any brand is its product or service. Whether you're creating a tangible product like skincare or clothing or offering a service such as consulting or personal training, the design process is critical. It's about bringing your idea to life in a way that resonates with your target audience while reflecting your brand's identity and values. This chapter will take a step-by-step approach to product or service design, from conceptualization to sourcing materials and testing to ensure you deliver something of real value.

Conceptualizing Your Product

Once you have a clear idea of your brand's purpose and identity, the next step is to translate that into a tangible product or service. This is where you start turning your abstract idea into something real that customers can experience.

Start with Your Brand's Purpose

Your product or service should be a direct extension of your brand's purpose. Ask yourself:

- **What problem is my product solving?**

- **How does my product reflect my brand's values?**

If your brand's mission is to offer eco-friendly solutions, your product must embody sustainability. If your purpose is to provide luxury experiences, your product should reflect that with high-end materials or premium service touches.

Sketching Your Idea

Before diving into technical details, start with simple sketches or outlines of your product or service. For physical products, this could be literal sketches or mood boards of how it might look, feel, or function. For services, it could be a flowchart that outlines the customer experience or journey.

Consider the following aspects:

- **Form and Function**: What will your product look like, and how will it work? If it's a service, how will it be structured and delivered?

- **User Experience**: How will the customer interact with your product? What emotions or reactions do you want them to feel when they use it?

- **Differentiation**: How will your product stand out from others on the market? This might come from innovative design, special features, or a unique customer experience.

Example:

If you're conceptualizing a line of organic skincare, your product idea could start with a simple sketch or description of your hero product, such as a face serum. You might decide it will be in eco-friendly packaging and formulated with rare botanical extracts that align with your brand's values of purity and sustainability. The user experience might focus on luxurious, spa-like application processes, giving customers a sense of indulgence.

Finding the Right Materials, Ingredients, or Resources

The quality of your product starts with the materials, ingredients, or resources you use. Whether you're sourcing raw materials for a physical product or gathering tools for a service, these choices should align with your brand's values and quality standards.

Sourcing for Physical Products

If you're creating a physical product, the materials and ingredients you choose will determine not only the functionality and durability of your product but also how well it reflects your brand's ethos. Here's how to approach sourcing:

1. **Align with Brand Values**: If your brand is eco-conscious, prioritize materials that are sustainably sourced, recyclable, or biodegradable. If your focus is on luxury, invest in premium materials that convey high quality.

2. **Research Suppliers**: Spend time researching and vetting potential suppliers. Look for suppliers who meet ethical standards, have certifications (e.g., organic, fair trade), and can provide consistent quality.

3. **Consider Cost and Scalability**: While using high-quality materials is important, you must consider your budget and whether your

suppliers can scale as your business grows. Aim for a balance between quality and affordability.

Sourcing for Services

For service-based businesses, your "materials" may include the tools, platforms, or technologies you use to deliver your service. For example, if you're offering a digital service, you'll need to invest in the right software or online platforms that allow you to deliver your service seamlessly.

1. **Choose the Right Tools**: Ensure the platforms or systems you choose are user-friendly, reliable, and scalable. For instance, if you're offering a coaching service, you may need video conferencing software, customer management systems, or scheduling tools that make it easy to deliver a smooth customer experience.

2. **Brand Alignment**: Just as with physical materials, your choice of tools should reflect your brand. For example, if your brand emphasizes innovation, choose cutting-edge technologies that enhance the user experience.

Example:

If you're launching an eco-friendly medspa, aligning with values like sustainability and convenience is important. Using eco-friendly, ethically sourced products can attract eco-conscious clients, while energy-efficient equipment and sustainable practices help reduce your environmental impact. An intuitive online booking system is key for a seamless customer experience, making it easy for clients to schedule treatments and payments. Customizing services to reflect client values, such as offering holistic, eco-conscious treatments, can also set your medspa apart and foster a loyal customer base.

Prototyping and Testing

Before launching your product or service, it's critical to test it to ensure it meets the needs of your target market. Prototyping allows you to create a working version of your product or service and gain valuable feedback before committing to large-scale production or launch.

Prototyping for Physical Products

Prototyping is the process of creating a sample or early model of your product to test its functionality, design, and user experience. This step helps identify any design flaws or areas for improvement before moving to production.

1. **Create a Prototype**: Depending on your product, a prototype can be a fully functional model or a simplified version that highlights the key features. For example, if you're developing a skincare or haircare line, you would create sample formulations, while in hospitality or wellness, you might develop sample spa products or wellness tools for testing.

2. **Test Functionality**: Ensure your product performs as intended. Does it meet customer expectations? Is it durable, reliable, and easy to use? For instance, in cosmetics, you would test for long-lasting wear or texture, while in hospitality, a prototype wellness treatment or in-room product would be evaluated for its effectiveness and customer satisfaction.

3. **Assess the User Experience**: Evaluate how potential customers interact with your product. Is it intuitive and user-friendly? In the wellness industry, you might test the ease of use of a massage oil or treatment device, while in skincare or cosmetics, you would assess application and feel on the skin.

4. **Gather Feedback**: Once your prototype is ready, test it with a small group of potential customers, friends, family, or selected target audience members. Collect feedback on what works, what doesn't, and how improvements can be made.

5. **Refine**: Based on the feedback, refine the product. Adjust the design, materials, or features as needed before moving into full production to ensure the highest quality.

Testing for Service-Based Businesses

For service-based businesses, thorough testing is essential to ensure smooth delivery and a positive customer experience.

1. **Pilot Your Service**: Offer a limited run of your service to a small group of beta customers. This is particularly important in the hospitality and wellness industries, where testing treatments, guest experiences, or wellness programs can reveal areas for improvement.

2. **Measure Performance**: Assess how well your service meets customer needs. Is it delivering the desired results? Are there any inefficiencies or pain points? In hospitality, this might involve evaluating the guest experience from check-in to check-out, while in wellness, you might assess the effectiveness of a service like a meditation class or spa treatment.

3. **Gather Customer Feedback**: After offering your service, gather feedback from your beta customers. What did they enjoy? Where can you improve? This insight is crucial to fine-tuning your service offering.

4. **Refine and Optimize**: Make necessary adjustments based on the feedback. Streamline processes, enhance service delivery, or simplify aspects that customers find confusing, ensuring your final offering is optimized for a seamless and valuable experience.

Bringing It All Together

Designing your product or service is where your brand truly begins to take shape. It's about taking your vision and making it a reality that aligns with your brand's identity, meets your customers' needs, and stands out in the marketplace. By carefully conceptualizing your product or service, sourcing the right materials or tools, and rigorously testing before launch, you're ensuring that what you bring to market is something you can be proud of, something that reflects the passion, quality, and purpose of your brand.

As you move forward to production and launch, remember that this is an ongoing process. Testing and refining doesn't end after the initial prototype—continuous improvement will be key to staying competitive and ensuring long-term success.

Chapter 4: Building a Brand Development Plan

Building a brand requires more than just creative ideas and a compelling story—it requires a clear and structured plan. A well-thought-out brand development plan not only guides you through the process of turning your idea into a reality but also helps you stay on track financially, operationally, and strategically. This chapter will walk you through creating a step-by-step brand development process, formulating your budget, and setting milestones and timelines to keep your project on course for a successful launch.

Creating a Step-by-Step Development Process

Building a successful brand involves multiple phases, each of which requires careful attention to detail. Structuring a step-by-step development process helps ensure that you move through each phase in an organized way and that nothing gets overlooked. Here's how to create a comprehensive plan from concept to inventory:

1. Concept Validation

This is the phase where you ensure your brand idea is viable. It's about assessing whether your product or service has a real market, aligns with your values, and meets consumer needs.

- **Market Research**: Analyze the industry trends, competition, and consumer demand to determine if your concept has potential.

- **Customer Feedback**: Reach out to your target audience, either through surveys or focus groups, to get feedback on your initial concept. This will help you refine your idea before moving forward.

2. Design and Development

Once you've validated your concept, it's time to bring it to life. In this phase, you will focus on developing the look, feel, and functionality of your product or service.

- **Product/Service Design**: Define the specifications of your product or service, whether it's the ingredients, materials, features, or delivery method. Collaborate with designers or developers to finalize the blueprint of your product.

- **Brand Identity**: Build the visual elements of your brand, including your logo, packaging, website, and other marketing materials. Ensure that these elements are cohesive and align with the values and personality of your brand.

3. Sourcing and Production

In this phase, you'll identify the suppliers or partners you need to manufacture or deliver your product or service.

- **Supplier Sourcing**: Identify and vet potential suppliers for materials, packaging, and production. Ensure they meet your quality standards and align with your budget.

- **Production Plan**: Once suppliers are selected, create a production schedule that outlines the timeline for manufacturing your product or preparing your service for delivery.

4. Quality Control and Testing

Before moving to full-scale production or launching your service, it's crucial to test everything to ensure quality and consistency.

- **Prototype Testing**: If you're creating a physical product, develop prototypes and test them for performance, durability, and customer satisfaction. If it's a service, pilot it with a select group of users to gather feedback and identify any issues.

- **Adjustments**: Based on the feedback from testing, make any necessary refinements to improve the final product or service.

5. Marketing and Branding Preparation

As you approach the launch phase, it's important to build excitement around your brand and ensure that all marketing materials are in place.

- **Marketing Strategy**: Develop a marketing plan that includes branding campaigns, social media outreach, email marketing, and influencer partnerships. Make sure your messaging aligns with your brand's values and resonates with your target audience.

- **Launch Materials**: Create all necessary marketing materials such as brochures, advertisements, website content, and social media posts. Ensure they're visually cohesive and reflect your brand identity.

6. Inventory and Distribution

Once your product or service is finalized, it's time to focus on getting it into the hands of customers.

- **Inventory Management**: For physical products, set up an inventory system to track your stock levels, ensuring you don't overproduce or underproduce. Use software to help manage orders, shipping, and returns.

- **Distribution Strategy**: Decide how you'll deliver your product or service to customers. Will you sell through an e-commerce platform, in brick-and-mortar stores, or directly through a service website?

Formulating Your Budget

Building a brand comes with financial considerations at every step, and a clear budget will help you avoid costly mistakes and keep your brand development on track. Formulating your budget requires careful planning and realistic goal setting.

1. Estimating Costs

Before you can set a budget, you need to estimate the costs for each brand development phase. Break down the costs into key categories, such as:

- **Product Development**: This includes design costs, prototyping, and any testing or adjustments needed before production.

- **Production and Sourcing**: Estimate the costs of materials, suppliers, and manufacturing. Don't forget to include packaging, shipping, and storage expenses.

- **Marketing and Branding**: Allocate funds for logo and brand design, website development, advertising, and other marketing efforts.

- **Operational Costs**: Include administrative costs like business registration, accounting services, and any tools or software you'll need to manage your business.

- **Distribution and Inventory**: Estimate the warehousing, shipping, and inventory handling costs.

2. Setting Realistic Financial Goals

Once you've estimated your costs, you can set realistic financial goals. This involves:

- **Sales Projections**: Based on your market research, estimate how much a product or service you expect to sell within a given timeframe (e.g., six months, one year). Use these projections to set revenue targets.

- **Profit Margins**: Calculate your profit margins by subtracting production and operational costs from your projected revenue. Ensure you set prices that cover your costs and allow for a healthy profit margin.

- **Break-even Analysis**: Determine your break-even point—the number of sales you need to make to cover all your expenses. This will give you a clear sense of when your brand will start turning a profit.

3. Funding Options

If your brand requires more capital than you currently have, there are various funding options to explore:

- **Self-funding**: If you have savings or personal assets, you may choose to self-fund the initial stages of your brand.

- **Small Business Loans**: Many entrepreneurs take out small business loans to cover start-up costs. Be sure to research loan options and understand repayment terms before committing.

    o **Revenue-based Business Funding**: https://davidallencapital.com/business-capital/aerdnaeiram

    o **Micro Funding**: https://davidallencapital.com/gigfunding/aerdnaeiram

    o **Business Line of Credit:** https://davidallencapital.com/line-of-credit/aerdnaeiram

- **Crowdfunding**: Platforms like Kickstarter or Indiegogo allow you to raise funds from supporters who believe in your idea. This option is especially useful for consumer-focused brands.

- **Venture Capital or Angel Investors**: If you need significant funding, you may consider seeking investment from venture capitalists or angel investors. Be prepared to present a detailed business plan and pitch your brand's potential for growth.

Setting Milestones and Timelines

A successful brand launch requires careful planning, which includes setting milestones and timelines. Establishing clear milestones helps you track progress and stay accountable to deadlines, while timelines ensure that each phase of development moves forward efficiently.

1. Identify Key Milestones

Milestones are the critical points in your brand's development that mark progress. These might include:

- **Concept Validation Complete**: When you've conducted market research and refined your brand idea.

- **Brand Identity Finalized**: When your brand name, logo, and visual elements are ready.

- **Product/Service Design Approved**: When your design is finalized and ready for production or service launch.

- **Production Begins**: When manufacturing starts or service infrastructure is in place.

- **Prototype Testing Complete**: When you've gathered feedback and made adjustments to your product or service.

- **Marketing Plan Executed**: When your marketing materials are ready and campaigns begin.

- **Launch Day**: When your product or service goes live and is available for purchase.

2. Create a Timeline

Once you've identified your key milestones, create a detailed timeline that includes deadlines for each phase. Start with your final launch date and work backward, setting realistic timeframes for each step in the process.

Here's a sample timeline for a product-based brand:

- **Month 1-2**: Concept validation and market research.
- **Month 2-3**: Product design and initial prototypes.
- **Month 3-4**: Brand identity design (logo, packaging, website).
- **Month 4-5**: Finalize suppliers and begin production.
- **Month 5-6**: Quality control and prototype testing.
- **Month 6-7**: Marketing and promotional planning.
- **Month 7-8**: Finalize inventory and distribution strategy.

- **Month 8 - 12**: Launch product and begin sales.

However, depending on the product type and if you opt to offer private label or custom develop your products, working with an experienced turnkey service consulting agency can drastically reduce your timeline to a matter of weeks.

3. Adjust as Needed

While having a timeline is essential, it's equally important to remain flexible. Challenges and delays are common in brand development, whether it's issues with suppliers, manufacturing setbacks, or unexpected marketing expenses. Be prepared to adjust your timeline when necessary, but always keep your milestones in sight to stay on track.

Bringing It All Together

Building a brand development plan is a strategic process that requires thoughtful planning and attention to detail. By creating a step-by-step development process, formulating a realistic budget, and setting clear milestones and timelines, you'll ensure that your brand moves forward with focus and efficiency. With each phase—concept validation, design, sourcing, testing, marketing, and launch—you'll inch closer to bringing your vision to life and introducing your brand to the world.

Chapter 5: Developing a Cohesive Brand Aesthetic

Your brand's aesthetic is more than just how things look; it's about the emotions, experiences, and perceptions that your visual elements evoke in your audience. A cohesive brand aesthetic not only makes your brand recognizable but also helps build trust and connection with your customers. Whether it's your website, product packaging, or social media, your brand's visual identity should consistently reflect its core values and personality.

This chapter will guide you through the key components of building a strong brand aesthetic, from crafting your visual identity to designing labels and packaging, and finally, working with designers or agencies to bring your vision to life.

Crafting Visual Identity: Colors, Typography, and Imagery

Your visual identity is a vital part of how your brand communicates with your audience. The right combination of colors, typography, and imagery can set the tone for your brand and create a lasting impression.

1. Choosing Your Brand Colors

Color is one of the most powerful tools in your brand's visual toolbox. Different colors evoke different emotions and associations, so it's essential to choose colors that align with your brand's personality and resonate with your target audience.

- **Understand Color Psychology**: Color can convey a wide range of emotions and messages. For example:

- **Red**: Excitement, passion, urgency.
- **Orange**: Playful, creative, enthusiastic.
- **Blue**: Trust, calm, professionalism.
- **Green**: Growth, sustainability, health.
- **Black**: Luxury, sophistication, power.
- **White**: Cleanliness, purity, freshness.
- **Yellow**: Optimism, warmth, happiness.
- **Gold**: Wealth, prestige, success.
- **Silver**: Introspection, intuition, uplifting.
- **Brown**: Stability, trustworthiness, comfort.
- **Gray**: Indifferent, neutral, balanced.
- **Purple**: Royalty, spirituality, luxury.
- **Pink**: Compassion, empathy, love.
- **Teal**: Tranquility, credibility, creativity.
- **Beige**: Adaptability, approachability, reliability.
- **Ivory**: Elegant, timeless, soothing.

Choose 2-3 primary colors that reflect your brand's core values. These will be used consistently across all your brand materials, from your website to packaging. You can also choose accent colors to use sparingly for highlights or special elements.

- **Be Consistent**: Once you've chosen your brand colors, use them consistently across all platforms and materials. This consistency will help create a recognizable and cohesive visual identity.

2. Selecting Typography

Typography, or font choice, plays a key role in setting the tone for your brand. Just like colors, fonts have their own personality, and the right choice can help reinforce your brand's message.

- **Match the Mood of Your Brand**: Think about the overall feeling you want your brand to convey. Serif fonts (like Times New Roman) tend to feel traditional and authoritative, while sans-serif fonts (like Arial) are often seen as modern and clean. Script fonts can feel elegant or playful, while bold, blocky fonts can give off a sense of strength or masculinity.

- **Choose a Readable Font**: Your primary font should be easy to read across different platforms, from digital screens to printed materials. Avoid fonts that are too decorative or hard to read, as this can make your brand seem less professional.

- **Font Pairing**: Many brands use a combination of fonts to create a dynamic visual identity. For example, you might use a bold sans-serif font for headings and a clean serif font for body text. Make sure your fonts complement each other without clashing.

3. Using Imagery to Reflect Your Brand's Personality

Imagery plays a critical role in shaping how customers perceive your brand. The photos, illustrations, and graphics you use should reflect your brand's values and resonate with your target audience.

- **Define Your Imagery Style**: Think about the types of images that will best represent your brand. For example:
    - **Minimalistic**: Clean, simple, and modern.
    - **Lifestyle**: Images that show your product being used in real-life situations.
    - **Bold and Graphic**: Eye-catching, colorful, and attention-grabbing.
    - **Natural and Organic**: Reflective of sustainability, nature, and health.

- **Consistency is Key**: Whether you're using stock photos or commissioning original photography, your imagery should feel consistent across all platforms. This helps create a unified brand experience, no matter where your audience encounters your brand.

Label and Packaging Design

Packaging and labeling are the first tangible touchpoints customers have with your product. A well-designed package can capture attention, communicate key information, and reinforce your brand identity. Here's how to create packaging and labels that stand out while staying true to your brand.

1. Align with Your Brand's Identity

Your packaging and labels should be an extension of your brand identity, using the same colors, typography, and imagery that you've chosen for the rest of your brand. Packaging is a powerful way to tell your brand's story visually.

- **Match the Product Experience**: If your product is premium and luxurious, your packaging should reflect that with elegant, high-quality materials like glass or metallic finishes. If your product is eco-friendly, consider using recycled or biodegradable materials and simple, earthy designs.

- **Design for Your Target Audience**: Always keep your target customer in mind when designing your packaging. If you're selling to a younger, trendier audience, bright colors and bold graphics might be the right fit. If your audience is more conservative or professional, a sleek, minimalistic design could be more appropriate.

2. Focus on Functionality

Beautiful packaging is important, but it must also be practical. Consider how your packaging will be used and displayed, both in stores and by customers.

- **Protect the Product**: Your packaging should protect your product from damage during shipping and handling. Ensure it is sturdy and fit for purpose.

- **Ease of Use**: Make sure your packaging is easy to open and use. If your product is a lotion, for example, consider a pump or squeeze bottle for convenience.

- **Sustainability**: Consumers are increasingly looking for eco-friendly options, so if possible, choose packaging that is sustainable, recyclable, or reusable.

3. Create Eye-Catching Labels

Labels should provide necessary information (such as ingredients or usage instructions) while also drawing the customer in. Here are some tips for creating effective labels:

- **Keep it Simple**: Don't overwhelm your customers with too much information. Highlight the key benefits of your product and keep the design clean and uncluttered.

- **Use Visual Hierarchy**: Make sure the most important information, such as your product name or key selling point, stands out by using larger fonts or contrasting colors.

- **Brand Consistency**: Your label should use the same colors, fonts, and style as your overall brand aesthetic. This ensures that your product looks like it belongs in your brand's family.

Working with Designers and Agencies

Bringing your brand's aesthetic to life often requires professional help, especially if you don't have a background in design. Working with designers or agencies can help you achieve a high-quality, polished look that reflects your brand's personality. Here's how to collaborate effectively with professionals.

1. Choosing the Right Designer or Agency

Not all designers or agencies will be the right fit for your brand. When choosing a partner, consider their style, experience, and ability to understand your vision.

- **Check Experience**: It's helpful to work with someone who has experience in your industry or with similar brands. They will be familiar with the best practices for packaging, labels, and visual identity specific to your niche.

- **Communication Skills**: A good designer or agency should be able to listen to your ideas and translate them into a visual concept. Make sure they are open to feedback and can communicate clearly throughout the process.

2. Communicating Your Vision

Clear communication is key to getting the results you want from your designer. Here's how to ensure you and your designer are on the same page:

- **Create a Brief**: Write a detailed design brief that outlines your brand's values, target audience, and visual preferences. Include examples of brands you admire, and describe the emotions or experiences you want your design to evoke.

- **Provide Feedback**: Throughout the design process, give constructive feedback. Be specific about what you like and don't like, and explain why. For example, instead of saying, "I don't like this color," say, "This color feels too bold for our brand. Can we try something softer that feels more calming?"

3. Staying on Budget

Design work can be expensive, so it's important to set a clear budget upfront. Make sure you and your designer agree on the scope of the project and the timeline to avoid any surprises.

- **Ask for a Detailed Quote**: Before the work begins, ask your designer for a breakdown of costs, including revisions. This will help you understand what's included in the price and what might cost extra.

- **Prioritize**: If you're working with a limited budget, prioritize the most important design elements first. For example, if your packaging is a critical part of your brand, focus on getting that right before spending money on additional marketing materials.

Bringing It All Together

A cohesive brand aesthetic is the visual embodiment of your brand's personality and values. By carefully selecting your colors, typography, and imagery, designing labels and packaging that align with your brand's identity, and collaborating effectively with professionals, you can create a strong, consistent aesthetic that resonates with your audience and sets your brand apart.

Chapter 6: Preparing for Production

Now that your brand identity, product design, and development plan are in place, it's time to prepare for production. This phase is critical to your brand's success—how you produce your products or deliver your services will directly impact your brand's reputation and profitability. A well-executed production plan ensures you deliver high-quality products efficiently, while keeping costs under control.

In this chapter, we will dive into the logistics of setting up your supply chain and inventory management, maintaining rigorous quality control, and choosing between outsourcing and in-house production. By the end of this chapter, you will have a solid understanding of how to structure and streamline your production process.

Setting Up Your Supply Chain and Inventory Management

A well-organized supply chain is the backbone of any successful production process. It ensures that you have the right materials, at the right time, in the right place. Efficient inventory management, on the other hand, helps you control costs, prevent shortages or overstocking, and meet customer demand.

1. Organizing Your Supply Chain

Your supply chain includes all the steps involved in getting your product from raw materials to the hands of your customers. It encompasses everything from sourcing suppliers to shipping and fulfillment. Here's how to build an efficient supply chain for your business:

- **Identify Key Suppliers**: Your suppliers are vital to your production process. You'll need to source materials, ingredients, or components from reliable suppliers who can meet your quality standards and timelines.

  When evaluating suppliers, consider:

  - **Reputation**: Look for suppliers with a proven track record of reliability and quality.

- **Pricing**: Ensure their pricing aligns with your budget and production goals.
- **Capacity**: Can the supplier handle the volume you expect to produce?
- **Sustainability and Ethics**: If your brand has ethical or sustainable values, ensure that your suppliers align with these principles.

- **Build Strong Relationships**: Maintain open and regular communication with your suppliers. Establishing strong relationships can lead to better pricing, improved service, and flexibility in case of unexpected changes in demand.

- **Set Up Shipping and Fulfillment Channels**: Determine how you will move your product through the supply chain, from production to your warehouse or directly to customers. Depending on your business model, you may need to work with logistics providers, freight companies, or third-party fulfillment centers.

2. Inventory Management Systems

Effective inventory management ensures that you have enough products to meet demand without overstocking, which ties up capital. Managing your inventory also helps avoid stockouts, which can damage customer satisfaction and loyalty.

- **Choose the Right Inventory System**: Inventory management software is crucial to tracking your products, managing orders, and controlling stock levels. Look for systems that integrate with your e-commerce platform or other business tools.

- **Cloud-Based Systems**: These allow real-time tracking and can automatically reorder materials or products when stock levels are low.
- **Barcode Scanning**: Many inventory systems offer barcode scanning for easy product tracking.

- **Set Up Reorder Points**: Calculate the minimum stock level for each product or material and establish reorder points. This ensures you don't run out of critical materials or finished products while keeping excess inventory low.

- **Safety Stock**: For key materials or products that are difficult to source or prone to supply chain disruptions, consider holding a small buffer of extra stock, known as safety stock, to protect against shortages.

Ensuring Quality Control

Consistent quality is essential to building a reputable brand. Customers expect the same level of quality each time they purchase your product, and even small deviations can harm your reputation. Implementing a rigorous quality control (QC) process ensures that your products consistently meet your standards.

1. Establish Quality Standards

Your quality standards should be based on your brand's core values and your target market's expectations. Quality standards should be well-defined and measurable whether you're producing beauty products, food, or clothing. Consider factors like:

- **Durability or Shelf Life**: How long should the product last? How will it hold up during use or storage?

- **Ingredients or Materials**: Are you using premium, natural, or sustainable materials? Ensure that each batch meets the required specifications.

- **Performance**: Does the product work as intended? Are customers getting the results they expect?

Once your standards are clear, document them for easy reference and make them part of your production process.

2. Developing a Quality Control Process

Quality control is a step-by-step process to verify that your products meet your established standards. It includes inspecting raw materials, monitoring production, and testing finished products.

- **Raw Material Inspection**: Before production starts, ensure that the materials or ingredients meet your specifications. Set criteria for accepting or rejecting batches from your suppliers.

- **In-Process Inspections**: During production, regular checks should be conducted to catch any issues early. This might include checking for defects, ensuring consistency in formulations, or verifying assembly quality.

- **Final Product Testing**: Before your product reaches the market, a final inspection or test should be performed. For physical products, this could include performance testing or appearance checks. For consumable products, such as food or cosmetics, testing might involve lab analysis for safety and regulatory compliance.

3. Continuous Improvement

Quality control isn't just about catching mistakes; it's about continually improving your processes. After each production run, review any quality issues that arose and determine how you can prevent them in the future. Create feedback loops with your production team and suppliers to ensure that quality problems are addressed quickly.

Outsourcing vs. In-House Production

One of the most important decisions you'll make is whether to produce your products in-house or outsource production to a third party. Both options have advantages and challenges, depending on your business model, product complexity, and resources.

1. Outsourcing Production

Outsourcing production involves partnering with a contract manufacturer or third-party company to produce your product. This option can be more cost-effective and allows you to focus on branding, marketing, and sales, while leaving the production process to experts.

- **Pros of Outsourcing**:

    o **Lower Upfront Costs**: You don't need to invest in manufacturing equipment, facilities, or staff.

    o **Scalability**: As your business grows, you can increase production without significant overhead costs.

    o **Expertise**: Third-party manufacturers often specialize in specific industries or product types, ensuring high-quality production.

- **Cons of Outsourcing**:

    o **Less Control**: You'll have less control over the production process, and any mistakes made by the manufacturer could reflect poorly on your brand.

- **Lead Times**: Depending on the manufacturer's schedule, you may face longer lead times for production.

- **Minimum Order Quantities (MOQs)**: Many manufacturers require you to order a minimum quantity of products, which can be a challenge for small businesses or startups.

2. In-House Production

In-house production means you control the entire manufacturing process, from sourcing raw materials to assembling the finished product. This option gives you complete control over quality and production timelines, but it comes with higher upfront costs and ongoing management challenges.

- **Pros of In-House Production**:

  - **Full Control**: You can oversee every aspect of production, ensuring that your product meets your quality standards.

  - **Flexibility**: You can make quick changes to the production process, whether it's adjusting a formula, changing a design, or experimenting with small-batch production.

  - **Brand Integrity**: In-house production can enhance your brand's authenticity, especially if your brand values craftsmanship or sustainability.

- **Cons of In-House Production**:

    o **High Upfront Costs**: Setting up production facilities, buying equipment, and hiring staff can be expensive.

    o **Operational Complexity**: Managing a production facility requires expertise in manufacturing, inventory management, and personnel.

    o **Capacity Limitations**: If your business grows rapidly, your in-house production may struggle to keep up with demand, requiring you to invest in additional capacity or staff.

3. Hybrid Approach

Some businesses choose a hybrid approach, handling some parts of production in-house while outsourcing others. For example, you might manufacture key components in-house but outsource packaging or final assembly. This allows you to retain control over the most critical aspects of your product while reducing overall production costs.

Bringing It All Together

Preparing for production is a complex but essential phase in building your brand. Setting up a robust supply chain and inventory management system ensures that your production process runs smoothly and efficiently. Implementing rigorous quality control measures helps maintain consistency and customer trust. Selecting the appropriate production method—be it outsourcing, in-house manufacturing, or a hybrid —will have a lasting impact on your brand's ability to scale and deliver high-quality products.

Chapter 7: Building Your Digital Presence

In today's marketplace, a strong digital presence is essential for the success of any brand. It's where your customers will first discover your products, interact with your brand, and make purchasing decisions. This chapter will guide you through the key components of building a powerful online presence: designing a user-friendly website, establishing a social media strategy, and leveraging email marketing to engage your audience and build loyalty.

Designing Your Website

Your website is the central hub of your digital presence. It's where potential customers will learn about your brand, explore your products or services, and ultimately make purchases. Designing a website that is both visually appealing and easy to navigate is crucial to creating a seamless experience that encourages visitors to stay, explore, and convert.

1. Brand-Aligned Design

Your website should be an extension of your brand identity. Every element—from colors and fonts to imagery and layout—should reflect your brand's personality and values. Here are some key points to consider:

- **Consistent Branding**: Use your brand's colors, fonts, and logo consistently throughout the site. This helps reinforce brand recognition and trust. Make sure the tone and voice of the copy align with your brand's personality.

- **Visual Aesthetics**: High-quality imagery, whether of your products, services, or brand story, is essential. Invest in professional photography or use stock images that align with your brand's look and feel. Visuals should enhance, not clutter, the user experience.

2. User Experience (UX)

A beautiful website is important, but it's equally important that visitors can easily navigate it. Good user experience (UX) design ensures that your visitors can find what they need quickly and without frustration.

- **Intuitive Navigation**: Your website should have a clear and straightforward menu. Avoid overwhelming visitors with too many options. Stick to essential categories like Home, About, Shop, Blog, and Contact. A search bar can be a helpful addition for larger websites.

- **Mobile Responsiveness**: With most web traffic now coming from mobile devices, it's vital that your website looks great and functions smoothly on smartphones and tablets. Responsive design automatically adjusts the layout and elements of your website to fit different screen sizes.

- **Loading Speed**: A slow website can turn visitors away. Optimize your site's loading speed by compressing images, minimizing code, and using reliable web hosting services. The faster your site loads, the more likely visitors are to stay and browse.

3. E-Commerce Functionality

If you're selling products or services online, your e-commerce functionality must be seamless and secure.

- **Product Pages**: Each product should have a dedicated page with detailed descriptions, high-quality images, and customer reviews. Provide essential information, like price, size, colors, ingredients, or materials, in a clear format.

- **Checkout Process**: Ensure the checkout process is easy to use, fast, and secure. Offer multiple payment options (credit card, PayPal, etc.) and minimize the number of steps required to complete a purchase. Provide clear shipping and return policies to build customer confidence.

- **Security**: Security is critical for e-commerce sites. Make sure your website uses SSL encryption (you'll know you have it if your URL begins with "https"), and display trust badges or certifications to reassure customers that their data is safe.

Establishing a Social Media Strategy

Social media is a powerful tool for building relationships with your audience, driving traffic to your website, and increasing brand awareness. To be effective, your social media presence should be intentional, consistent, and aligned with your overall brand identity.

1. Choosing the Right Platforms

Not all social media platforms are created equal, and your brand doesn't need to be on every single one. Focus on the platforms where your target audience spends the most time.

- **Instagram**: Ideal for visually-driven brands, especially those in fashion, beauty, wellness, and lifestyle. Instagram is a great platform for sharing product images, behind-the-scenes content, and engaging stories.

- **Facebook**: Facebook is useful for reaching a broad demographic and is especially effective for running targeted ads. It's also a good platform for community building through groups and events.

- **TikTok**: If your brand targets a younger audience, TikTok's short-form video format can help you reach and engage Gen Z consumers.

It's great for showcasing creativity, tutorials, and viral trends.

- **LinkedIn**: For B2B businesses or brands that cater to professionals, LinkedIn is a must. It's a platform for thought leadership, networking, and industry insights.

- **Pinterest**: Pinterest is another visual platform, perfect for brands in home decor, fashion, beauty, or DIY sectors. It's an excellent place to showcase visually appealing products and drive traffic back to your website.

2. Creating Engaging Content

Content is the lifeblood of social media. To keep your audience engaged, you need to regularly post content that resonates with them and aligns with your brand's values and message.

- **Educational Content**: Share tips, tutorials, and how-tos that relate to your products or industry. For example, a beauty brand could post skincare routines, while a fitness brand could offer workout tips.

- **Behind-the-Scenes Content**: Give your audience a peek behind the curtain by showing them how your products are made, what goes on in the office, or the story behind your brand. This humanizes your brand and builds a deeper connection with followers.

- **User-Generated Content (UGC)**: Encourage customers to share their own photos or videos of your products. This not only builds social proof but also fosters a sense of community. Highlight user-generated content on your brand's social media and thank customers for their contributions.

- **Consistent Posting**: Consistency is key to maintaining an active and engaged following. Create a content calendar to schedule your posts, plan ahead, and ensure you're regularly engaging with your audience.

3. Engagement and Community Building

Social media is not just a broadcasting tool; it's a platform for two-way communication. Engage with your followers by responding to comments, messages, and mentions.

- **Host Giveaways or Contests**: These can be a fun way to increase engagement and grow your following. Make sure the prizes are relevant to your brand, and encourage participants to share your content to maximize visibility.

- **Collaborate with Influencers**: Partnering with influencers in your industry can give your brand credibility and expose it to a broader audience. Choose influencers whose values align with your brand for authentic promotion.

Email Marketing and Content Creation

Email marketing is one of the most effective ways to nurture relationships with your audience, drive sales, and build long-term brand loyalty. It allows you to communicate directly with your customers in a more personalized way.

1. Building Your Email List

Before you can start sending emails, you need to build a list of subscribers who are interested in your brand.

- **Opt-In Forms**: Place email opt-in forms throughout your website—on the homepage, in blog posts, and as pop-ups. Offer an incentive, like a discount, free shipping, or a free guide, in exchange for signing up.

- **Lead Magnets**: Lead magnets are valuable resources that entice visitors to join your email list. These can include e-books, exclusive tutorials, checklists, or other downloadable content related to your brand.

2. Creating Engaging Email Content

Your email content should be relevant, valuable, and engaging to your subscribers. The goal is to build a relationship over time, not just bombard them with sales pitches.

- **Welcome Series**: When someone first subscribes to your email list, send them a series of welcome emails. Introduce your brand, share your mission, and offer a discount or special offer to encourage their first purchase.

- **Regular Newsletters**: Send out a regular newsletter to keep your audience up to date on new products, promotions, or brand news. Make sure each email offers value—whether it's a helpful tip, an inspiring story, or exclusive content.

- **Segmented Email Campaigns**: Segment your email list based on subscriber behavior (such as purchase history, location, or engagement level) and tailor your emails accordingly. This allows you to send more personalized and relevant content to different groups of subscribers.

3. Automated Email Sequences

Automation allows you to send emails based on specific triggers, such as when someone signs up, abandons their cart, or makes a purchase.

- **Abandoned Cart Emails**: If a customer leaves items in their cart without completing the purchase, an automated reminder email can nudge them to return and complete the transaction. Offering a small incentive, like free shipping or a discount, can boost conversion rates.

- **Re-Engagement Emails**: If subscribers haven't opened your emails in a while, send them a re-engagement campaign to bring them back into the fold. You can offer a special promotion or ask for feedback on why they've been inactive.

Bringing It All Together

Building a digital presence is an ongoing process that requires a clear strategy, consistent effort, and regular updates. Your website is the foundation of your online brand, providing a user-friendly, brand-aligned experience for customers. Social media allows you to connect with your target audience and build a community around your brand, while email marketing helps nurture those relationships and drive sales over time.

By focusing on these key elements—website design, social media strategy, and email marketing, you'll create a cohesive digital presence that engages your audience, builds loyalty, and drives long-term success for your brand.

Chapter 8: Launching Your Brand

Launching your brand is one of the most exciting and critical phases in your entrepreneurial journey. It's the culmination of your hard work, creativity, and planning, and it's your chance to make a memorable first impression on your target audience. This chapter will guide you through crafting a robust launch plan, building strategic partnerships, and leveraging public relations to maximize your brand's visibility.

Crafting a Launch Plan

A well-structured launch plan is essential for generating buzz and ensuring that your brand reaches its target audience effectively. Here's how to craft a comprehensive launch plan:

1. Setting Launch Goals and Objectives

Begin by defining clear goals and objectives for your launch. These should be measurable and time-bound, helping you track your progress and success.

- **Sales Targets**: Set realistic sales goals for the first month, quarter, or year. Consider factors such as your marketing budget, audience size, and previous engagement metrics.

- **Brand Awareness**: Determine how you will measure brand awareness, such as tracking social media followers, website traffic, or email subscribers.

- **Media Coverage**: Aim for specific press mentions, features, or reviews within a certain timeframe post-launch.

2. Creating a Pre-Launch Timeline

Timing is critical when it comes to building anticipation for your launch. Create a detailed timeline leading up to the launch date, breaking down tasks and deadlines into manageable segments.

- **Pre-Launch Activities**: Use the weeks leading up to the launch to build excitement. Activities could include teaser campaigns on social media, sneak peeks of your products, or countdown posts that engage your audience and encourage sharing.

- **Content Calendar**: Develop a content calendar that outlines what, when, and where you'll post about your launch across different platforms. This ensures that your messaging is cohesive and aligned across channels.

3. Developing Key Messaging

Craft compelling messaging that communicates your brand story, values, and unique selling propositions (USPs). This messaging should resonate with your target audience and be adaptable for different platforms and formats.

- **Elevator Pitch**: Create a succinct elevator pitch that clearly articulates what your brand offers and what sets it apart. This will be useful for networking, media outreach, and promotional materials.

- **Taglines and Hashtags**: Develop a catchy tagline and relevant hashtags to promote your launch on social media. Make sure these are easy to remember and reflect your brand's personality.

4. Planning Launch Day Activities

Decide how you will officially launch your brand. This could involve a virtual or in-person event, promotional offers, or live product demonstrations.

- **Launch Event**: If you choose to host a launch event, plan all details, including location, format (in-person, virtual, or hybrid), activities, and how to invite guests (influencers, customers, media). Make it engaging and consider incorporating interactive elements like Q&A sessions or giveaways.

- **Promotions and Discounts**: Consider offering launch promotions or limited-time discounts to incentivize early purchases. This can create urgency and encourage people to try your products.

Building Partnerships and Collaborations

Strategic partnerships can amplify your launch visibility and extend your reach into new audiences. Here's how to leverage partnerships effectively:

1. Identifying Potential Partners

Look for businesses, influencers, or organizations that align with your brand values and target audience.

- **Complementary Brands**: Seek out brands that offer complementary products or services. For example, if you're launching a skincare line, consider partnering with a beauty influencer or a wellness brand.

- **Local Businesses**: Collaborate with local businesses to create joint promotions or events. This not only supports your local community but can also help you tap into established customer bases.

2. Creating Win-Win Collaborations

When approaching potential partners, highlight the mutual benefits of collaboration.

- **Cross-Promotion**: Offer to feature their products in your promotional materials, and in return, ask them to promote your launch to their audience. This could be done through email newsletters, social media shoutouts, or blog features.

- **Joint Events**: Host joint events, whether virtual or in-person, to draw in audiences from both brands. This could include co-hosting a webinar, a product launch party, or an Instagram Live session.

Public Relations and Media Outreach

Leveraging public relations (PR) effectively can significantly boost your brand's visibility and credibility during the launch. Here's how to maximize your PR efforts:

1. Crafting Your Press Kit

A well-prepared press kit is essential for media outreach. It should include:

- **Press Release**: Write a compelling press release that highlights your brand, products, and launch event. Make it newsworthy by focusing on unique aspects, such as innovative product features, sustainability efforts, or community engagement.

- **Background Information**: Include background information about your brand, its mission, and the story behind your products. This helps journalists understand your brand's narrative.

- **Visual Assets**: Provide high-quality images, logos, and any other visual assets that journalists may need for their articles. Having these ready makes it easier for them to feature your brand.

2. Targeting the Right Media Outlets

Research and compile a list of media outlets, bloggers, and influencers that cover your industry.

- **Local Media**: Don't overlook local newspapers, magazines, and blogs, which can be very effective in spreading the word within your community.

- **Industry Publications**: Target publications and websites that specialize in your niche. These outlets often have dedicated readers who are more likely to be interested in your products.

3. Conducting Outreach

When reaching out to media contacts, personalize your communication and clearly articulate why your story is relevant to their audience.

- **Email Pitching**: Send personalized email pitches to journalists and bloggers. Keep your pitch concise and engaging and make it easy for them to see the newsworthiness of your launch.

- **Follow-up**: If you don't receive a response, consider following up after a week or so. A polite reminder can help keep your brand on their radar.

4. Engaging with Influencers

Consider partnering with influencers in your niche to further amplify your launch efforts.

- **Product Seeding**: Send free products to influencers in exchange for honest reviews or social media posts. This can create organic buzz and expose your brand to their audience.

- **Sponsored Content**: Collaborate with influencers for sponsored posts or stories that align with your launch. Make sure their style and audience match your brand.

Bringing It All Together

Launching your brand is a significant milestone that deserves careful planning and execution. By crafting a thoughtful launch plan, building strategic partnerships, and effectively leveraging public relations, you can create buzz and excitement around your brand, ensuring a successful launch.

As you prepare to step into the spotlight, remember that this is not just the end of a process but the beginning of your brand's journey. Stay agile and responsive to feedback and be ready to adapt your strategies as you learn more about your customers and the market.

Chapter 9: Scaling and Growing Your Business

As an entrepreneur, launching your brand is just the beginning of your journey. The next exciting phase is scaling and growing your business, which requires a strategic approach and a willingness to adapt. In this chapter, we will discuss how to analyze feedback to refine your brand, expand your product line for diversification, and build a strong team and infrastructure to support your growth.

Analyzing Feedback and Adjusting

Customer feedback is a goldmine for understanding your market and refining your offerings. Actively seeking and analyzing feedback can help you improve your products, enhance customer satisfaction, and drive future growth.

1. Collecting Customer Feedback

Gathering feedback can be done through various channels, ensuring you receive a comprehensive view of customer sentiments.

- **Surveys and Questionnaires**: Use online tools like Google Forms or SurveyMonkey to create surveys that customers can fill out post-purchase. Ask specific questions about their experience, product satisfaction, and areas for improvement.

- **Social Media Engagement**: Monitor comments, direct messages, and mentions on social media. Engage with your audience by asking open-ended questions and encouraging discussions about your products and brand.

- **Product Reviews**: Pay attention to reviews on your website, third-party platforms, or social media. Both positive and negative reviews provide valuable insights into customer preferences and pain points.

2. Analyzing Feedback Data

Once you've collected feedback, it's essential to analyze the data effectively.

- **Identifying Trends**: Look for common themes in the feedback. Are customers consistently praising a particular product feature? Are there frequent complaints about the same issue? Identifying trends will guide your improvements.

- **Quantitative Analysis**: Use data analysis tools to track quantitative metrics, such as satisfaction ratings, Net Promoter Scores (NPS), and engagement levels. This numerical data can help you assess overall customer sentiment.

- **Qualitative Insights**: Combine quantitative data with qualitative insights from open-ended responses to gain a holistic view of customer perceptions. This depth of understanding will guide your decision-making.

3. Implementing Changes

Feedback is only valuable if you act on it. Create an action plan based on the insights gathered.

- **Prioritizing Improvements**: Focus on areas that align with your business goals and have the most significant impact on customer satisfaction. Consider the resources required for each improvement and their potential ROI.

- **Testing Changes**: Before fully implementing major changes, consider running pilot tests. This allows you to gauge customer reactions without a full commitment.

- **Communicating Updates**: Share updates with your customers about changes made based on their feedback. This transparency fosters a sense of community and shows that you value their input.

Expanding Your Product Line

Once your brand is established and you've gathered valuable customer insights, consider expanding your product line to drive growth and meet evolving market demands.

1. Conducting Market Research

Before expanding, conduct thorough market research to identify new opportunities.

- **Analyzing Customer Needs**: Use the feedback collected to determine what additional products or services your customers want. Are there gaps in your current offerings that you can fill?

- **Exploring Trends**: Stay informed about industry trends and consumer behavior. Research competitors to see what products are gaining traction in the market.

- **Testing New Concepts**: Before fully launching a new product line, consider creating prototypes or samples and testing them with a select group of customers. This can provide valuable insights and reduce the risk of a full-scale launch.

2. Strategic Product Development

Plan for growth and diversification by strategically developing your product line.

- **Complementary Products**: Consider launching products that complement your existing offerings. For example, if you sell skincare, you might introduce a complementary line of beauty tools.

- **Seasonal or Limited-Edition Products**: Create seasonal products or limited-edition items to generate excitement and urgency among your customers. This can also help you assess demand for potential permanent additions to your product line.

- **Diversification**: Explore completely new product categories or markets. This requires careful research and understanding of the new target audience to ensure alignment with your brand.

3. Marketing New Products

A successful launch of new products is as crucial as the initial brand launch.

- **Building Anticipation**: Use your existing marketing channels to build excitement around new product launches. Teasers, behind-the-scenes content, and influencer partnerships can create buzz.

- **Cross-Promotion**: Promote new products alongside your existing offerings. Bundling products together can encourage customers to try new items while enhancing their overall shopping experience.

- **Gathering Feedback**: After launching new products, continue to collect feedback to evaluate their performance and gather insights for future improvements.

Building a Team and Infrastructure

As your business grows, it becomes essential to build a strong team and infrastructure that can support your expanding operations.

1. Identifying Key Roles

Assess the roles necessary for your business as it scales.

- **Core Functions**: Identify which functions are essential for daily operations and long-term growth, such as marketing, sales, customer service, and production.

- **Skill Gaps**: Analyze your current team's skills and identify any gaps that need to be filled. Consider what expertise is necessary to support new product launches or marketing strategies.

2. Hiring Strategies

Develop a hiring strategy that aligns with your business goals and culture.

- **Defining Roles Clearly**: Create clear job descriptions that outline responsibilities, qualifications, and expectations. This helps attract the right candidates.

- **Cultural Fit**: Look for candidates who align with your brand values and company culture. A cohesive team that shares a vision will work more effectively together.

- **Freelancers vs. Full-Time**: Decide whether to hire full-time employees or leverage freelancers/contractors for specific projects. This can provide flexibility while you assess the need for permanent staff.

3. Establishing an Organizational Structure

Create an organizational structure that promotes efficiency and communication.

- **Hierarchy**: Determine how to structure your team to facilitate clear communication and accountability. This could involve defining leadership roles and reporting structures.

- **Collaboration Tools**: Implement collaboration tools and project management software to streamline communication and ensure everyone is aligned on tasks and deadlines.

4. Investing in Training and Development

As your team grows, prioritize ongoing training and development to ensure your staff is equipped to support the business.

- **Skill Development**: Offer training programs and workshops to enhance employees' skills and keep them up-to-date with industry trends.

- **Encouraging Innovation**: Foster a culture of innovation by encouraging team members to share ideas and contribute to product development or marketing strategies.

Bringing It All Together

Scaling and growing your business is an ongoing journey that involves analyzing feedback, expanding your product line, and building a capable team. By continuously refining your offerings based on customer insights, strategically diversifying your products, and establishing a strong organizational infrastructure, you can position your brand for long-term success.

As you navigate this growth phase, remain adaptable and open to change. The market is dynamic, and your ability to pivot and respond to new challenges will ultimately define your brand's trajectory.

Chapter 10: Navigating Regulatory Compliance and Certification for Custom Formulation and Private Label Products

When developing and selling custom-formulated or private-label organic and natural products, whether they are over-the-counter (OTC) drugs, skincare, cosmetics, wellness supplements, or alcoholic beverages, it is crucial to comply with a range of federal, state, and certification requirements. Operating outside these regulations can result in severe penalties, product recalls, or even the closure of your business. This chapter will cover the various regulatory bodies, their certification requirements, and the importance of working with an experienced consulting agency like Redefine Beauty ID Consulting to ensure compliance and streamline your production process.

Key Regulatory Agencies and Certification Bodies

1. The U.S. Food and Drug Administration (FDA)

The FDA is the primary federal agency regulating the safety, quality, and labeling of cosmetics, OTC drugs, dietary supplements, and some alcoholic products. Businesses engaged in custom formulation and private-label production must comply with the FDA's guidelines and obtain specific certifications or licenses.

Licensing and Certification Requirements for Manufacturers

- **FDA Registration**: Manufacturing facilities that produce OTC drugs, cosmetics, dietary supplements, or other FDA-regulated products must be registered with the FDA under the **Voluntary Cosmetic Registration Program (VCRP)** for cosmetics and the **Drug Establishment Registration** for OTC drugs.

- **Good Manufacturing Practices (GMP) Certification**: To ensure product safety and quality, manufacturers of OTC drugs, supplements, and cosmetics must adhere to **Current Good Manufacturing Practices (cGMP)**. GMP certification involves rigorous inspections of the facility to confirm that manufacturing processes meet the standards for cleanliness, quality control, and consistency. This is essential for any business selling supplements, skincare, or drug-related products.

- **Facility Inspections and Audits**: The FDA can conduct regular inspections of manufacturing facilities to ensure they comply with these standards. Non-compliance can lead to warnings, fines, or shutdowns.

- **Product Labeling and Claims**: Manufacturers must also ensure that their products are correctly labeled. Claims such as "organic," "natural," or "cruelty-free" must comply with federal definitions. Misleading labels can result in violations, fines, and product recalls.

Over-the-Counter (OTC) Drugs

For OTC products such as sunscreen, acne treatments, or anti-dandruff shampoos, specific **Drug Establishment Registration** is required, and the products must comply with **OTC Monograph** guidelines.

2. U.S. Department of Agriculture (USDA)

The USDA regulates organic products through its **National Organic Program (NOP)**. For manufacturers and businesses producing organic products, such as skincare, supplements, and even alcoholic beverages, obtaining organic certification is crucial.

Licensing and Certification Requirements for Organic Products

- **Organic Certification**: To label products as "organic," businesses must obtain certification from a USDA-accredited organic certifying agent. This process ensures that the ingredients and production methods meet USDA organic standards, including the prohibition of synthetic chemicals, pesticides, and GMOs.

- **Organic Handler Certification**: Facilities that process, package, or distribute organic products must also obtain an **Organic Handler Certification**. This certification ensures that products maintain their organic integrity throughout the supply chain.

- **Inspection and Compliance**: Regular inspections are conducted to verify that the production process complies with organic standards. Failure to comply can lead to the loss of organic certification and legal penalties.

3. Leaping Bunny Certification (Cruelty-Free)

Leaping Bunny certification is the gold standard for cruelty-free products, verifying that no animal testing was conducted at any stage of the product's development. Cosmetics, skincare, and other personal care products can obtain this certification to appeal to ethically conscious consumers.

Certification Requirements for Cruelty-Free Products

- **Certification Process**: Businesses must apply for Leaping Bunny certification, which includes a comprehensive audit of supply chains and ingredient sourcing to ensure no animal testing occurs.

- **Supply Chain Auditing**: All ingredient suppliers must also comply with cruelty-free standards, and businesses must submit to annual audits to maintain certification.

- **Marketing Benefits**: Leaping Bunny certification allows businesses to use the recognizable logo on product packaging, offering a powerful marketing advantage in the cruelty-free market.

4. Alcohol and Tobacco Tax and Trade Bureau (TTB)

For those in the business of private label or custom formulation of alcoholic beverages like wine, beer, and spirits, the TTB governs production, labeling, and advertising.

Licensing and Certification Requirements for Alcoholic Beverages

- **Basic Permit**: To legally produce, bottle, or sell alcoholic beverages, businesses must first obtain a **Basic Permit** from the TTB. This permit is required for producers, wholesalers, and importers of wine, spirits, and beer.

- **Labeling and Formula Approval**: Every alcoholic product must have its label and formulation approved by the TTB. The **Certificate of Label Approval (COLA)** ensures that the product meets federal labeling requirements, such as alcohol content, health warnings, and ingredient transparency.

- **State Licensing**: In addition to federal TTB requirements, most states require businesses to apply for additional licenses to produce and sell alcohol. Some states may also have stricter regulations regarding production methods or distribution.

5. State-Level Regulatory Requirements

State-level regulations vary significantly depending on the type of product. Skincare, cosmetics, supplements, and alcohol often require additional state-specific licenses or registrations.

State Licensing for Cosmetics and Skincare Products

Some states, like California, require cosmetic manufacturers to register their products with the state's Department of Public Health. Businesses must ensure compliance with both state and federal guidelines to operate legally.

State Licensing for Alcoholic Beverages

Many states have their own Alcohol Beverage Control (ABC) boards, which may require separate licensing, inspections, and tax filings in addition to federal TTB regulations.

The Importance of Adhering to Regulatory Compliance

Operating outside the bounds of federal and state regulations can result in severe consequences, including:

- **Fines and Penalties**: Non-compliance can lead to significant fines, sometimes reaching millions of dollars depending on the severity of the violation. For example, the FDA and USDA impose substantial fines for misbranding, mislabeling, or falsely claiming organic certification.

- **Product Recalls**: In the event of non-compliance, regulatory bodies like the FDA can mandate product recalls, leading to financial loss and damage to your brand's reputation.

- **Facility Shutdowns**: Manufacturing facilities that fail inspections or do not meet GMP or safety standards can be shut down by regulatory agencies, severely disrupting business operations.

- **Loss of Certifications**: Businesses that fail to maintain USDA organic or Leaping Bunny cruelty-free certifications will lose the ability to market their products as such, which can harm their market positioning and customer trust.

Benefits of Working with AERDNA EIRAM

Navigating the complex regulatory landscape for custom formulations and private-label products can be overwhelming. AERDNA EIRAM offers **solutions** to help you manage the compliance process seamlessly while simultaneously working with you on building your business and developing and launching your new product brand.

Comprehensive Compliance Support

When applicable, AERDNA EIRAM assists with every aspect of regulatory compliance, including FDA registration, GMP certification, USDA organic certification, and TTB licensing for alcoholic beverages to include your state ABC board. Our team is experienced in managing both federal and state-specific requirements, ensuring that your business operates within the law.

Labeling and Certification Expertise

From securing USDA organic and Leaping Bunny certifications to ensuring your product labeling complies with FDA regulations, AERDNA EIRAM streamlines the process, minimizing the risk of errors that could lead to fines or product recalls.

Supply Chain Auditing and Quality Assurance

We work with you to ensure your supply chain meets all regulatory requirements, conducting thorough audits to verify the safety, quality, and ethical sourcing of your ingredients and materials.

Final Thoughts

Navigating the regulatory requirements for custom formulation and private-label products is a complex yet crucial aspect of building a successful brand. Adhering to federal, state, and local regulations ensures that your products are safe, ethical, and legally compliant, protecting your business from fines, product recalls, and reputational damage. By partnering with AERDNA EIRAM, you can confidently move through the regulatory process, secure in the knowledge that your brand is built on a solid foundation of compliance, quality, and ethical standards.

Chapter 11: Staying True to Your Brand

As your business continues to grow and evolve, staying true to your brand becomes increasingly important. Maintaining brand integrity, building long-term customer relationships, and adapting to market changes without losing your identity are essential to fostering a loyal customer base and ensuring your brand's longevity. This chapter explores these key aspects of brand management.

Consistency is Key

Consistency is a cornerstone of successful branding. It establishes trust and recognition in the minds of consumers, and it is vital for maintaining your brand's integrity as you scale.

1. Defining Your Brand Elements

To maintain consistency, clearly define the core elements of your brand:

- **Brand Voice and Messaging**: Establish a consistent tone and messaging style that reflects your brand's personality. Whether it's professional, friendly, or quirky, ensure that all communications, from social media posts to customer emails, adhere to this voice.

- **Visual Identity**: Your logo, color palette, typography, and imagery should be used consistently across all platforms. Create brand guidelines that outline how these elements should be applied in different contexts.

- **Customer Experience**: Consistency extends beyond visuals and messaging; it includes the entire customer experience. Ensure that the quality of your products and services meets the expectations set by your brand promises.

2. Implementing Brand Guidelines

Develop comprehensive brand guidelines to serve as a reference for your team and any external partners.

- **Creating a Brand Manual**: Include details on your brand's mission, vision, values, target audience, and unique selling propositions. This document should also cover dos and don'ts for using brand assets and messaging.

- **Training and Onboarding**: Provide training sessions for new team members to familiarize them with your brand guidelines. This ensures that everyone in your organization understands the importance of maintaining consistency.

3. Monitoring Brand Representation

Regularly monitor how your brand is represented across various channels and platforms.

- **Social Media Monitoring**: Keep an eye on how your brand is being discussed and portrayed on social media. Tools like Hootsuite or Sprout Social can help you track mentions and sentiment.

- **Customer Feedback**: Actively seek feedback from customers about their experiences with your brand. This can help you identify areas where consistency may be lacking and address any discrepancies promptly.

Building Long-Term Customer Relationships

Fostering customer loyalty and retention is essential for sustaining growth. Building long-term relationships with your customers can transform them into brand advocates who promote your brand to others.

1. Creating Exceptional Customer Experiences

Strive to provide exceptional customer experiences at every touchpoint.

- **Personalization**: Use customer data to personalize communications and offers. This could include personalized emails, product recommendations, or loyalty rewards tailored to individual preferences.

- **Responsive Customer Service**: Provide timely and empathetic responses to customer inquiries and complaints. Effective communication can turn negative experiences into positive ones, reinforcing customer loyalty.

2. Implementing a Loyalty Program

Develop a customer loyalty program that rewards repeat purchases and encourages engagement.

- **Points-Based System**: Consider implementing a points-based loyalty system where customers earn points for each purchase, which can be redeemed for discounts or exclusive offers.

- **Referral Incentives**: Encourage customers to refer friends and family by offering incentives for successful referrals. This not only rewards loyal customers but also helps you expand your customer base.

3. Engaging with Your Community

Build a community around your brand by engaging with your customers beyond the point of sale.

- **Social Media Engagement**: Actively engage with your audience on social media platforms by responding to comments, sharing user-generated content, and hosting giveaways or contests.

- **Exclusive Events**: Consider hosting exclusive events, such as product launches, workshops, or webinars, to strengthen your connection with customers and make them feel valued.

Embracing Evolution without Losing Identity

In a dynamic market, change is inevitable. The ability to adapt to new trends and consumer preferences while staying true to your core brand values is crucial for long-term success.

1. Identifying Core Values

Clearly define your brand's core values and mission. These should remain unchanged, serving as a guiding light as you navigate evolution.

- **Mission Statement**: Regularly revisit your mission statement to ensure it still reflects your purpose. This statement should resonate with both your team and customers.

- **Value Alignment**: Ensure that any new products, services, or marketing strategies align with your core values. This consistency reinforces your brand identity and builds trust.

2. Gathering Market Insights

Stay informed about market trends and consumer behavior to identify areas for evolution.

- **Regular Research**: Conduct regular market research and competitor analysis to understand emerging trends and consumer needs. This can help you anticipate changes and adapt proactively.

- **Customer Feedback Loops**: Continue gathering feedback from customers to gauge their responses to changes. Implementing a feedback loop allows you to stay attuned to their evolving preferences.

3. Implementing Changes Thoughtfully

When introducing changes, do so thoughtfully to minimize the risk of alienating your existing customer base.

- **Incremental Changes**: Consider making incremental changes rather than sweeping overhauls. This allows you to test new ideas while maintaining your established identity.

- **Communicating Changes**: Be transparent with your customers about why changes are being made. Share the thought process behind new products or initiatives and how they align with your brand's evolution.

Bringing It All Together

Staying true to your brand while navigating growth and change is vital for long-term success. By ensuring consistency across all brand elements, building strong relationships with customers, and embracing evolution without compromising your core values, you can create a resilient brand that stands the test of time.

As you continue your entrepreneurial journey, remember that your brand is not just a product or service, but an experience shaped by your customers.

Reflect, Refine, and Reignite

As you stand at the conclusion of this journey through the various stages of building your brand, it's essential to recognize that this is not merely an end but a stepping stone to an ongoing adventure in entrepreneurship. Reflecting on your experiences, refining your strategies, and reigniting your passion for your brand will be pivotal as you continue to navigate the dynamic landscape of business. This concluding chapter will explore the ongoing journey of entrepreneurship and emphasize the individuality of your brand.

Chapter 12: Conclusion - The Ongoing Journey of Idea to Inventory

Entrepreneurship is often likened to a marathon rather than a sprint. It requires endurance, resilience, and a constant desire to improve and innovate. Here are some key strategies to stay motivated throughout this journey:

1. Embrace the Long-Term Perspective

While the excitement of launching your brand may fade, it's crucial to maintain a long-term perspective.

- **Set Incremental Goals**: Break down your larger vision into smaller, achievable goals. Celebrate each milestone, whether it's a successful product launch, reaching a sales target, or receiving positive customer feedback. These small victories will help keep your motivation high.

- **Stay Committed to Your Vision**: Revisit your mission and vision regularly. Reflecting on why you started can reignite your passion during challenging times. Keep these values at the forefront of your decision-making.

2. Cultivate a Support System

The entrepreneurial journey can be isolating, but surrounding yourself with a supportive network can provide motivation and encouragement.

- **Join Entrepreneurial Communities**: Engage with local or online entrepreneurial communities. Sharing experiences, challenges, and successes with like-minded individuals can provide inspiration and accountability.

- **Mentorship**: Seek out mentors who have experience in your industry. Their guidance can provide valuable insights and keep you motivated as you navigate the ups and downs of entrepreneurship.

3. Prioritize Self-Care

Taking care of your physical and mental well-being is essential for sustaining motivation.

- **Work-Life Balance**: Strive for a healthy work-life balance to prevent burnout. Schedule regular breaks and time for personal interests, family, and friends to recharge your energy.

- **Mindfulness Practices**: Consider incorporating mindfulness practices, such as meditation or journaling, into your routine. These can help you stay centered and focused amid the challenges of entrepreneurship.

4. Adapt and Learn

The entrepreneurial landscape is ever-changing, and flexibility is key to maintaining motivation.

- **Stay Curious**: Cultivate a mindset of continuous learning. Attend workshops, read books, or take online courses to stay informed about industry trends and enhance your skills.

- **Embrace Failure as Learning**: Accept that setbacks are a natural part of the entrepreneurial journey. Rather than viewing failures as roadblocks, see them as opportunities for growth and learning.

Your Brand, Your Way

Celebrating your success is essential, but equally important is recognizing the individuality of your brand. Your brand is a reflection of your unique vision, values, and the journey you have undertaken. Here's how to embrace your brand's uniqueness and celebrate your achievements:

1. Acknowledge Your Growth

Take time to reflect on how far you've come since the inception of your brand.

- **Document Your Journey**: Keep a journal or a visual timeline of your brand's development. Documenting your milestones, challenges, and victories will provide a tangible reminder of your hard work and growth.

- **Celebrate Achievements**: Regularly celebrate achievements, both big and small. Whether it's launching a new product, hitting a sales goal, or receiving positive feedback, acknowledging these moments reinforces your commitment to your brand.

2. Tell Your Brand Story

Your brand's story is a powerful tool for connecting with your audience.

- **Share Your Journey**: Use your platforms—whether social media, newsletters, or your website—to share your story. Highlight the challenges you've overcome, your passion, and what makes your brand unique. Authentic storytelling fosters a deeper connection with your audience.

- **Engage Your Audience**: Encourage your customers to share their experiences with your brand. User-generated content and testimonials not only promote your products but also reinforce the community aspect of your brand.

3. Stay Authentic

As you scale and evolve, remain true to your brand's core identity.

- **Refine, Don't Redefine**: As you adapt and grow, focus on refining your brand rather than redefining it. Ensure that any new products, services, or strategies align with your core values and mission.

- **Maintain Your Brand Values**: Your brand values should guide all decision-making processes. By staying committed to your principles, you reinforce your brand's authenticity and integrity.

Bringing It All Together

The journey of entrepreneurship is an ongoing adventure filled with opportunities for reflection, refinement, and reignition. By embracing a long-term perspective, cultivating a supportive network, prioritizing self-care, and celebrating your unique brand, you position yourself for continued success.

As you move forward, remember that your brand is a reflection of your passion, purpose, and individuality. Each step you take will shape your journey, and by staying true to your vision, you will not only achieve your goals but also create a meaningful impact in the lives of your customers.

Your entrepreneurial journey is uniquely yours, celebrate it, learn from it, and let it inspire others. Embrace the journey ahead with enthusiasm and determination, and watch as your brand continues to evolve, thrive, and resonate with those you serve.

Working with a Consulting Agency

At AERDNA EIRAM, we understand that every entrepreneur's journey is unique. Our mission is to empower you to bring your brand vision to life by providing turnkey and comprehensive services tailored to your business needs. Whether your project is just a concept or fully realized, it can be a long journey filled with twists and turns, often confusing and stressful as you navigate industry-specific compliance and regulations. Here's how we can assist you:

1. AERDNA EIRAM Services

Our consulting services are designed to meet you where you are in your brand-building journey.

AERDNA EIRAM offers:

- **Business Funding**: Access financial resources and guidance to secure the capital necessary for your business growth.

- **Commercial Real Estate Funding**: Access to financial capital necessary to purchase and build out your commercial property.

- **Commercial Real Estate Locating**: Get expert assistance in finding the ideal location for your business, tailored to your specific needs and budget.

- **Start-up Business Formation and Development**: Navigate the complexities of starting and operating your business with our support in legal requirements, structure, registration, and operations. Work with us to identify growth opportunities, optimize operations, and develop strategies that drive your business forward.

- **Manufacturing and Supplier Liaison**: Benefit from our connections and expertise in sourcing reliable suppliers and managing manufacturing processes.

- **Brand Concept and Development**: Collaborate with our experts to craft a cohesive brand identity, encompassing your brand story, personality, and core values.

- **Custom Formulation and Private Label Product Development**: From concept to production, we guide you through sourcing quality materials and managing each stage of product development.

- **Website, Catalog, and Flipchart Design and Development:** We design highly functional and informative websites, catalogs, and flipcharts featuring your products and services.

- **PR Marketing Campaign Strategy**: We create compelling and impactful marketing strategies that resonate with your target audience and boost your brand visibility.

- **Ghostwriting and Copywriting**: Access professional writing services to craft compelling content that reflects your brand voice and message without the need for personal authorship.

3. Ongoing Support

Our commitment to your success doesn't end with the launch of your brand. We provide ongoing support and consultation as your business grows and evolves.

You're Officially Ready To Bring Your Vision To Life

The journey of entrepreneurship is filled with learning, growth, and opportunities for innovation. With the tools and resources outlined, you are well-equipped to navigate the complexities of building your brand. Whether you choose to work with AERDNA EIRAM or utilize your newly acquired tips of the trade and fly solo, remember that each step you take brings you closer to realizing your vision.

Your brand journey is unique, and it deserves to be celebrated. As you move forward, reflect on your experiences, refine your strategies, and reignite your passion. The entrepreneurial world is dynamic, and with the right tools and resources at your disposal, you can adapt and thrive in any environment. Embrace the challenges and triumphs ahead, and continue to shape your brand in a way that reflects your individuality and vision.

www.ingramcontent.com/pod-product-compliance
Lightning Source LLC
Chambersburg PA
CBHW070153230526
45471CB00002B/640